W9-DEL-085

Neil and His Meal Mobile

Anders Hanson

Consulting Editor, Diane Craig, M.A./Reading Specialist

ABDO Publishing Company

Published by ABDO Publishing Company, 4940 Viking Drive, Edina, Minnesota 55435.

Printed in the United States.

Credits
Edited by: Pam Price
Curriculum Coordinator: Nancy Tuminelly
Cover and Interior Design and Production: Mighty Media
Photo and Illustration Credits: BananaStock Ltd., Brand X Pictures, Corbis Images, Digital Vision, Hemera, Image 100, Image Ideas, Image Source, Tracy Kompelien, Stockbyte

Library of Congress Cataloging-in-Publication Data

Hanson, Anders, 1980-
    Neil and his meal mobile / Anders Hanson.
      p. cm. -- (Rhyme time)
    Includes index.
    ISBN 1-59197-808-4 (hardcover)
    ISBN 1-59197-914-5 (paperback)
    1. English language--Rhyme--Juvenile literature. I. Title. II. Rhyme time (ABDO Publishing Company)

PE1517.H378 2004
428.1'3--dc22
                                                                    2004050793

SandCastle™ books are created by a professional team of educators, reading specialists, and content developers around five essential components that include phonemic awareness, phonics, vocabulary, text comprehension, and fluency. All books are written, reviewed, and leveled for guided reading, early intervention reading, and Accelerated Reader® programs and designed for use in shared, guided, and independent reading and writing activities to support a balanced approach to literacy instruction.

Let Us Know

After reading the book, SandCastle would like you to tell us your stories about reading. What is your favorite page? Was there something hard that you needed help with? Share the ups and downs of learning to read. We want to hear from you! To get posted on the ABDO Publishing Company Web site, send us e-mail at:

sandcastle@abdopub.com

SandCastle Level: Fluent

Words that rhyme do not have to be spelled the same. These words rhyme with each other:

cartwheel

mobile

deal

peel

feel

real

ideal

squeal

meal

steel

MEAL MOBILE

This card game is almost over.

Jeffrey will **deal** the cards for the next game.

Brittney likes gymnastics.

She can do a **cartwheel**.

Eric and Stefan think a day spent at the beach is **ideal**.

Dogs are Lana's favorite animals.

She likes how soft and cuddly they **feel**.

Carson's family is having a
barbeque for their evening **meal**.

Brody is eating a banana.

Soon all that will be left is the **peel**.

Vic and Rob paint action figures.
They try to make them look **real**.

It is time for Lacey to take a nap.

She will watch her **mobile** until she falls asleep.

When the piglet is picked up,
it lets out a **squeal**.

Diane and Alexandria climb on a **steel** jungle gym.

Neil and His Meal Mobile

It's hard for some people
to cook a real meal.

Captain Neil will solve this ordeal
in a way that's ideal.

He will kindly make each meal
and deliver it in his
new, blue meal mobile.

His first stop is the home
of his neighbor, Camille.

She is so happy to see Neil
that she lets out a really big squeal.

Neil brings Camille
a yummy hot meal
that has great appeal.

Neil likes the way helping
people makes him feel.

He's so happy
that he does a cartwheel.

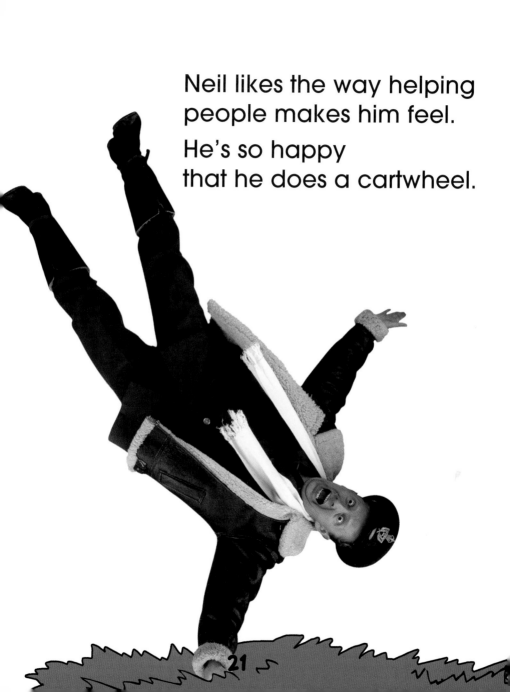

Rhyming Riddle

What do you call a perfect gymnastics move?

Ideal cartwheel

Glossary

cartwheel. a handspring where the body turns over sideways with the arms and legs spread out

ideal. completely or highly satisfactory, the best of its kind

mobile. an artistic device with parts that are arranged so they will move in the air currents

ordeal. a difficult or painful experience

steel. a strong, hard metal made from iron

About SandCastle™

A professional team of educators, reading specialists, and content developers created the SandCastle™ series to support young readers as they develop reading skills and strategies and increase their general knowledge. The SandCastle™ series has four levels that correspond to early literacy development in young children. The levels are provided to help teachers and parents select the appropriate books for young readers.

Emerging Readers
(no flags)

Beginning Readers
(1 flag)

Transitional Readers
(2 flags)

Fluent Readers
(3 flags)

These levels are meant only as a guide. All levels are subject to change.

To see a complete list of SandCastle™ books and other nonfiction titles from ABDO Publishing Company, visit www.abdopub.com or contact us at:
4940 Viking Drive, Edina, Minnesota 55435 • 1-800-800-1312 • fax: 1-952-831-1632